W9-BYZ-561

Praise from participants who have benefited from Steven Gaffney's seminars and the strategies contained within these pages.

"I would recommend Steven Gaffney's programs to any organization wishing to bring honesty, open communication and personal empowerment to its staff. By way of an afternoon seminar, Steven helped us distinguish what people value most— how to manage expectations for results and listen proactively to accomplish our goals together. I saw changes in my staff's behavior and our bottom line almost immediately. If you want a program that can really make a difference in both the attitude of your staff and the performance of your organization, Steven's are the perfect choice."

Gary Helminski, managing director and senior vice president, **3D International**

"Steve has helped us tremendously to address our company's organizational structure and future growth. He truly offers the best course that training money can buy."

Juanita Pappert, senior human resource manager and assistant vice president, **SAIC**

"Steven, your presentation was excellent! After attending, I immediately began to implement some of your helpful communication techniques to facilitate teamwork. I also began incorporating strategies that I believe enhance my own methods of communication. Thanks for your useful tips, Steve. They will last a lifetime."

Sallie Wiley, employee development specialist, **Office of Personal Management**

"Steven's unique approach to customer service has provided our Help Desk employees with the expertise and confidence to handle incoming calls and requests in a highly professional manner. His course has dramatically improved the level of effectiveness and efficiency with which we can respond to our customers

Shelby Hill, help desk training manager,
Marriott International

"Our staff signs up for Steven's course because of his topic and delivery. He has a reputation for being knowledgeable, compassionate and sincere. His charisma inspires the audience to utilize his life-changing message."

Lisa Heiser, career management director for faculty and staff, **The Johns Hopkins University**

"In my seven years with SAIC, this is by far the best course I have ever attended. Steve delivered the course material in a manner that kept my attention the entire time. He shared real-life situations in which the information he delivered could be applied. As a result, I feel that I will, without a doubt, be able to communicate not only more effectively, but also more efficiently. I am usually not this excited about seminars such as this, but what Steven presented has really impacted my life."

Chris Cobb, strategies group subcontract manager, **SAIC**

"50 percent of the attendees were promoted to higher level management positions. Many of them learned to successfully confront and overcome obstacles by implementing Steven's techniques."

Gretchen VonGehren, vice president, marketing, **American Express**

"Excellent!! I loved it! I have never attended a course as helpful as this one promises to be."

Sherri Glover, contract specialist,
U.S. Department of the Interior

"This is the most valuable training class I have ever attended. As a result, I am a better team leader and relate to my colleagues at a profoundly higher level. I expect to significantly reduce complaining in our department by 75%. Meetings will be shorter and more productive by eliminating 25% of unnecessary information. Many colleagues anticipate improvements in their working relationships after learning Steven Gaffney's realistic and straightforward communication techniques. This course can increase the efficiency of managers and staff at all levels."

Brian Twillman, training coordinator,
Environmental Protection Agency

"Excellent. Good mix of personal experience, mini exercises and audience participation with a common-sense approach. Introducing these communication strategies to our TQL teams should result in a minimum 50 percent savings in the development of products and applications."

Patti Sturges, program coordinator, **Litton**

"One of the best presentations we have ever had! Our sales force is thrilled with the practical tools and messages from Steven that will enable them to produce great results. Our administrators are extremely pleased to see the sales staff respond positively to Steven's messages about being proactive and taking accountability."

Nicholas Ramfos, chief administrator,
Alternative Commuter Programs

"The seminar was outstanding! There is no way to leave without learning something. I'd recommend that every analyst, including my own, attend this training."

Geri Young, senior. purchasing,
Marriott International

"We found Steve to be motivating and highly effective in helping our organization to rededicate itself to providing excellence in customer service."

Thomas Pogue, administrator,
Department of Public Works and Transportation

"I recommend this class to every employee because it is the best I have ever taken in my career. It has really helped me to improve my communication skills."

Cindy Abbruzzese, software engineer, **Telecordia**

"Steve's classes are phenomenal organizational and personal development tools. They never fail to raise the achievement and potential of every attendee."

Cora Carmody, chief information officer,
Litton PRC

"Best course I've ever taken. More than 60 percent of the employees in my division took the course on their own time and all responded that it was a very worthwhile experience. In addition to boosting morale, the course has increased the flow of direct, positive communication among our employees, saving us time and getting us faster results."

Steve Fusco, division manager
and vice president, **SAIC**

JUST BE HONEST

Authentic Communication Strategies That Get Results and Last a Lifetime

STEVEN GAFFNEY

JMG Publishing, Arlington Virginia

JMG Publishing
Arlington, Virginia

Printed in the United States of America
ISBN 0-9715377-1-2

Current Printing (last digit) 10 9 8 7 6 5 4 3 2 1

Book design and production by Hannah Kleber
Cover photo by Clay & Company, Clay Blackmore
Cover design © 2002 TLC Graphics, www.TLCGraphics.com

Norman Cousins said,
"Death is not the greatest loss in life,
the greatest loss in life is
what dies within us while we live."

So, this book is dedicated to
everyone who has something to say
but isn't saying it.

And to my family and friends,
you mean the world to me.

ACKNOWLEDGEMENTS

With a great deal of concern about missing someone,
I would like to thank the following people (not in any
particular order) who have made a huge difference in the
creation of this book:

All of the participants of my seminars and keynote
addresses, for providing me with so many wonderful and
insightful anecdotes.

My business director, Marisa Andrews, who does so many
excellent things, including prodding me to do this project.
Truth be told, she insisted that I get some form of a book
done. Without her, who knows when something would
have happened.

Theo Androus, who, besides being one of my closest
friends, contributed through his writing and editing.

Bill Cates, who contributed through his coaching, advice,
and encouragement which was invaluable to completing
this project.

Brad Blanton, the author of *Practicing Radical Honesty:
How to Complete the Past, Live in the Present* and
Build a Future with a Little Help From Your Friends
(Sparrowhawk Press, 2000) for teaching me the
distinction between notice and imagine, as well as
the basis for the notice versus imagine exercise.

My parents, Marina and John Gaffney, who edited this book when I did not know where else to turn.

Juanita Pappert, who has contributed through her friendship, tireless support of, and belief in this work.

Mike Casey, who, besides being one of my closest friends, helped me formulate some of the ideas in this book.

Gary Helmenski, who was the first person who believed I could make it as a professional speaker and seminar leader... even when I did not believe it myself.

My family and friends, for always being there with their love and support, even when they doubted and were scared for me.

CONTENTS

Introduction

Why Read This Book?

While most of us are able to speak, many of us struggle to communicate.

Consider your relationships, both personal and professional. Do you ever feel misunderstood or frustrated by others? Do you have any difficult people in your life? Is there a professional colleague, friend, family member, or significant other with whom you have struggled? Are there problems that continue to remain unresolved despite your best efforts? Do you avoid saying important things for fear of creating a conflict? Do you feel that other people avoid saying other things for fear of creating conflict?

The bottom line is that every dimension of our lives is affected by our ability to communicate with others and their ability to communicate with us. This ability to communicate is directly impacted by the level of honesty we share with them.

How much time have we wasted? How many opportunities for happiness, success, and love have we squandered, because of a lack of honesty in our communications with others? How often have we jumped to the wrong conclusions and allowed ourselves to get upset before we had all the facts? And how often have we been on the receiving end of the same thing?

Have you ever attended a meeting or had a conversation that felt like a waste of time? One where you weren't even sure what the purpose was, let alone why you needed to be there? One where someone said one thing, then turned around and did exactly the opposite? Why does this happen? Why are people unable or unwilling to speak up? What are they avoiding? What is this costing in time, stress and missed opportunities?

This Book Has Answers

Go to any bookstore, and you'll find plenty of books on how to outsmart difficult people from your spouse to your children to your co-workers — how to wheedle, cajole, lead, or fool them into doing what you want them to do.

If those books are working for you, then keep reading them. But if you want a book about how to be honest with people and how to have them be honest with you simply and effectively, then I challenge you to read this book. The ideas, strategies, and techniques presented here really work. Not all of them come naturally, and you may not love every one; however, the issue is whether or not they work. They do.

This book will show you how to communicate and produce immediate and dramatic results with anyone, regardless of their backgrounds, needs, personalities or personal agendas. You will receive the keys to learn how to eliminate communication breakdowns and personality conflicts with even the most difficult people; prevent problems before they happen; and get the bottom line results you desire at work and at home.

In addition you will learn specific strategies, techniques, and tools to:

- Eliminate repetitive issues and time wasted in conversations and meetings

- Alleviate the debilitating stress caused by personality conflicts and unresolved issues

- Compel others to be honest with you

- Get the information you need to effectively do your job and accomplish your goals

- Have people do what they say they will do and have deadlines be met consistently

- Help you give and receive feedback without being defensive

- Express your true emotions effectively, even anger

- Prevent problems that cause projects and contracts to fail

- Resolve personality differences and create more successful relations, even with people who are negative or on whom you have given up

- Give you back unlimited time, energy, and money now wasted on communication breakdowns

This book will help you cut through the confusion that so many "self-help" books cause, helping you create effective, productive, and honest relationships no matter how time-impoverished, overworked, understaffed, or under-resourced you and those around you may be.

Although this book describes many work-related situations, its lessons and its message about honest communication can be applied to personal relationships as well. The anecdotes you read are true, but names, occupations, and some details have been changed to protect identities.

CHAPTER I
THE SECRET TO COMMUNICATING EFFECTIVELY

Have you ever felt like someone wasn't being totally honest with you?

According to the book *The Day America Told the Truth* 91 percent admitted that they lie regularly—*91 percent*. Now that may seem high, but think about it for a moment.

It is possible to lie by what we choose to say, but it is also possible to lie by what we choose not to say. We have all lied, no matter what reason we used to excuse the behavior to ourselves. I believe the biggest reason that people lie is fear. Some common fears that may motivate a person to lie are fear of alienating someone, fear of rejection, and fear of retribution. As individuals are unique, so are their fears.

We all have heard that honesty is the best policy, but it often seems easier to lie than to speak the truth. Many people tend to rationalize by saying, "It's no big deal," "I can handle it," or "It's not worth bringing up." We tend to believe that the cost of addressing an issue is greater than the cost of not addressing it. But is that really the case? Unfortunately, it has been my experience in working with thousands of people, that most us are not aware or *choose* not to be aware of an unresolved issue's true cost.

The Cost of Communication Breakdowns

Become aware of the hidden costs, and then choose what *you* will do.

TIME

Almost two months of productivity per employee are lost each year due to communication issues. That's one out of every six days! Now, that's a big deal, since most of us never feel like we have enough time as it is.

How much time do you spend thinking about a problem you are having? Does it take you longer to complete tasks because of your preoccupation with this issue? Have you ever caught yourself staring off into space, daydreaming about how you wish you *could* deal with the situation? Do you ever reread a document or e-mail many times because you are looking for the "real" meaning? Do you spend time wondering what other people think about you and/or the job you are doing? Has a project ever taken more time than it should have because you did not receive all of the information necessary to complete it?

CONFIDENCE & MOTIVATION

Are you allowing an issue from your past to affect your confidence and willingness to take initiative in the present? Are you allowing a particular issue to affect your willingness to confront or resolve other issues? Does thinking about it drain you, make you sad, or rob you of the ability to live your life as you deserve and desire?

Relationships With Others

Does an unresolved issue affect your relationship with other people? Do you lash out at people who are unrelated to the problem? Are you allowing work issues to affect your relationships at home? Are you allowing your issues at home to affect your relationships at work? Are unresolved issues accumulating with someone to the point where you feel disconnected from them?

Teamwork

It is estimated that 80 percent of work-related problems are due to lack of open, honest communication. Is an unresolved problem affecting the members of your team and their ability to work together? Are people withholding information? Do meetings last beyond their allotted time and fail to accomplish their objectives because people aren't handling the real issues? Are the "real" meetings going on outside the meetings? Are people talking about someone behind his or her back instead of talking directly to that person? How is this affecting your workload, productivity, and effectiveness?

Turnover

Detailed exit interviews conducted with departing employees by human resource professionals reveal that problems arising from poor or dishonest communication is the number one reason why employees leave an organization. This is responsible for as much as 75 percent of employee turnover. People frequently say they are leaving because of money, but they often don't want to state the true reason for fear of burning their bridges behind them. How many people have left your organization because of issues with others? What is this costing you in time, stress, and productivity as you train new people and wait for them to get up to speed with their workload?

STRESS AND QUALITY OF LIFE

Have you ever found yourself unable to concentrate on those around you because you were preoccupied with an unresolved issue? At dinner with your loved ones or friends, have you ever watched their lips move but failed to hear a single word they were saying? Do you toss and turn in bed, unable to fall asleep because of an unresolved problem? Are you feeling fatigued and lethargic? Have you ever felt as though the "weight of the world" was upon your shoulders? Have you ever squandered a weekend or a vacation because, while you were there *physically*, you were unable to be there mentally?

If you answered yes to even *one* of these questions, then the costs of not resolving an issue/problem in your life are mounting. All of this affects your productivity, morale, job satisfaction, and overall happiness.

I challenge you to "try on" that the cost of resolving an issue/problem is minimal when compared to the cost of not resolving it. When you do have the necessary conversation to resolve it, you will be amazed by how relieved you feel and by how this affects every dimension of your life.

Two Common Strategies That Don't Work

Time and increasing communication are two common strategies we use to resolve issues, but they are usually ineffective.

TIME

Some people rationalize by saying, "Time heals all wounds." Yes, on occasion, we may want to give an issue some time before attempting to resolve it. That may be wise to gain *perspective* on the issue, but not to *resolve* and get beyond it. If time really healed all wounds, people would not blame their inability to take effective action in the present on issues stemming from childhood and other events in the past as often as they do.

In fact, time can deceive us into thinking that the issues with a person have been handled. However, all it usually takes is seeing or conversing with that person or being in a situation that reminds us of our past, for us to go right back to being as upset as we were before.

INCREASE COMMUNICATION

Another way we typically try to resolve communication issues is by simply *increasing the amount and modes of communication.*

For example, what is the typical response when there is a problem in the workplace? *Let's have a meeting and talk more about it.* How many times have you had to sit through one of those painful meetings in which someone is just pontificating and regurgitating what someone else said, just to make themselves look good?

Afterward, you think to yourself, "We got so sidetracked, what did we accomplish?" This is the soap opera concept of meetings. You go to a meeting, you might miss a couple of meetings, and then you go to the next one, and it is as if you never missed any at all. It is staggering to think of the money and time lost in unproductive meetings.

Consider this: if the key were simply to *increase the amount* of communication, you would think that the use of e-mail, cell phones, fax machines and pagers would have reduced communication problems, right?

Wrong! In spite of all of these extra tools we have available to help us increase the "quantity of communication," it seems as if there are *even more* misunderstandings, mistakes, and conflicts than *ever before*. And what is really astonishing is that despite having all these tools to communicate, people still complain that they don't have the necessary feedback to do their jobs properly.

Consider our children. How many children do you see walking around with cell phones and pagers their parents gave them? Yet, we are having even more problems with our children than ever before.

You might be wondering if I am saying that cell phones, pagers and e-mail are bad. The answer is no. What is wrong is the way we are *using* them. Increasing communication, as well as the channels to communicate, is not *the* answer.

The Solution

Honest, "effective" communication is *the secret* to working effectively with anyone. In the following chapters, I will provide tips and techniques that will revolutionize the way you communicate with every single person in your life. The only thing you have to do is be willing to learn a new and better way of doing things.

CHAPTER 2
THE MOST CRITICAL KEY TO HONEST COMMUNICATION

The most critical strategy for honestly communicating and working effectively with anyone is simple, yet it is *the* key to resolving the most difficult problems in less time and with greater skill. It is *the distinction between what we "notice" and what we "imagine."* I was first introduced to this concept by Dr. Brad Blanton, whose new book is *Practicing Radical Honesty: How to Complete the Past, Live in the Present and Build a Future with a Little Help from Your Friends*.

For our purposes, the word "notice" refers to the *facts of the situation*, and the word "imagine" refers to *everything else that goes on in our heads*—our opinions, assumptions, and judgments.

Let's look at some quick examples:

You notice that someone has on a red tie, and you imagine that the tie is fashionable. Someone else might notice the tie, but imagine it is *not* fashionable.

You notice that someone is wearing jeans on a business casual day, and you may imagine that it's appropriate attire. Someone else might notice the jeans but imagine it is inappropriate attire.

You notice someone came in 30 minutes late to the staff meeting, and you may imagine that the person just forgot about the meeting. Someone else might notice that the person came in 30 minutes late and imagine that he doesn't care about the meeting

You notice that someone did not say that they appreciate you, and you imagine that they don't like or care about you. Someone else might imagine that the person is overworked or is just uncomfortable voicing his or her appreciation.

Is it possible to notice someone's attitude or personality? The answer is no, you can only imagine that. But, you can notice their behavior, which may or may not accurately reflect their moods. For instance, simply because someone is smiling, would you automatically imagine that they are feeling positive or happy? How many times have you hidden your true feelings behind a smile?

All we can truly "notice" about someone is what is universally accepted as fact, such as appearance, words, and action. Everything else is imagination: opinions, judgments, evaluations, and assumptions.

Simple, But Not Easy

By now, you can probably see the problem: People confuse their *imagination* with what they *notice*. In other words, they think their opinions are facts. Not recognizing the difference between the two often leads to trouble.

> A couple of years ago, I took boxing lessons. My instructor was also a promoter for some local boxing events. One day he approached me and, knowing I

was a professional speaker, asked if I would be willing to announce a boxing event he was promoting. Thinking it would be fun and different, I agreed.

As unbelievable as it may seem, during the middle of the second bout, the former heavyweight champion of the world, Mike Tyson, entered the building.

I noticed that Mike Tyson walked in with a group of people, circled the seating area, went into the locker room area, and finally sat in the front row.

I had never announced a boxing event, and I had never met Mike Tyson. So, not knowing what to do, I went over to him and introduced myself as the announcer and asked him if he'd like to come up into the ring after the next bout to say a few words to the crowd. He replied, "No man, I'm afraid to go into the ring." Mike Tyson afraid to be in a boxing ring? I imagined he was kidding.

Right before the seventh and final bout, the promoter asked me to announce the presence of Mike Tyson and some local celebrities and to invite them to come into the ring.

As soon as I announced Tyson's name, I heard someone yelling at me. I looked over in the direction of the voice. And there he was, Mike Tyson, the former heavyweight champion of the world, signaling me over.

Now, many of you would have probably thought, "Oh no! Danger! Danger!" But not me... I innocently and naively walked over to him with microphone in hand and asked him what he wanted. He replied, "I told you not to introduce me."

And no, I did not try to be a communication seminar leader and say, "You sound mad. Do you want to talk about it?" Instead, fearing for my life, I took full responsibility and simply said, "I'm sorry."

Unfortunately it didn't end there. Mike Tyson then decided to come into the ring. I don't know if you can imagine what it feels like to have Mike Tyson about 10 feet away from you, *in a boxing ring*, yelling and pointing at you. But the value of having adult diapers was coming to mind.

Eventually, he cooled off and left the ring. While I was understandably relieved, I still did not know why he had reacted the way he did.

I later found out that after the infamous ear-biting incident, he was banned from being in any boxing ring. He took that *very* seriously, so when I asked him to come up to the ring, he was trying to politely handle the situation by saying that he was afraid. When I ignored his wishes and announced his name anyway, he "imagined" I was disrespecting him and responded accordingly.

A few days later, my boxing instructor came to me and said, "I heard Mike Tyson told you not to announce his name, so why did you announce it anyway?" I told my instructor that I thought Mike Tyson was kidding. He replied, "Why on earth would you think *that* guy was kidding?"

My instructor had a point. Have you ever been in a situation where you missed all the warning signs?

I noticed that Mike Tyson said "I'm afraid to go into the ring," and I imagined he was kidding. Only my imagination lived for me as a fact. In other words, I wrongly thought that it was a fact that he was kidding, so I did not even think to check in with my imagination or to ask him for clarification.

Now, some of you may say, "Well, Mike Tyson should not have acted that way." But the point is that I single-handedly could have avoided the entire situation if I had checked in with my imagination by asking him whether or not he was serious.

We all have to deal with people who can be extremely difficult. But we have the power to handle a lot of difficult situations if we check in with our imaginations before we take action.

How many times have you been mistaken about something that you could have sworn was true? I have observed countless examples of executives and managers who lead with their imaginations rather than the facts. Problems regarding motivation, initiative, feedback, and customer service—all completely avoidable—occur because people do not check in with their imaginations. Let's explore how something so simple could affect so many different areas of our lives.

Motivation

How often do you see people trying to motivate others by
what *they* imagined would be motivating?

Susan, a manager at a major telecommunications
company, recently shared with me her attempts to
motivate her group. The group had to complete a
critical project on a tight deadline. Susan promised
them they could have the following Friday off if the
project was completed on time. Everyone began
working harder, except for Roger. So, Susan began
to constantly remind Roger about the day off, hoping to increase his productivity. Finally, Roger told
her, "I am not interested in receiving Friday off. If I
am home on Friday, I'll have to clean out the garage.
I would rather be working at the office." So, by
attempting to use what she *imagined* would be a good
motivator for *everyone*, Susan had accomplished just
the opposite with Roger.

Initiative

Imagination can cripple us if we are not careful. It not only
affects our interaction with others, but it can also significantly alter our careers. Let's review an example.

Janice, a financial analyst, stopped taking leadership
roles because of her imagination. Her boss, Ed, told
her she would be in line for a promotion within a
couple of months. Several months passed without
any discussion of the promotion. Janice imagined
that her boss must have changed his mind. So, in

retaliation, she stopped assuming a leadership role and performed only the necessary tasks associated with her position.

Finally, after a year of resentment and mediocrity, she decided to confront Ed about being overlooked for the position. He was genuinely surprised and said he would have promoted her a long time ago, but he assumed she would not want the promotion because of the extra hours it required. Since Ed had noticed Janice complaining about already working long hours and not having enough time with her family, he imagined she would not be interested in being promoted. Frustration on Janice's part appeared to Ed to be a lack of initiative. A simple conversation could have prevented this. Instead valuable resources went untapped, hard feelings were harbored, and nobody won.

Feedback

How often have you seen someone refuse to deal with an issue or a problem because they *imagine* that addressing it would result in negative repercussions?

I have often observed managers and executives wrongly conclude that the person who is offering negative feedback is simply a troublemaker or a disgruntled employee. The reality is that this person is often the only team member who is willing to be brave enough to speak up. Management incorrectly assumes that nobody else feels the same way and comes down hard on the perceived malcontent. If the others witness the boss harshly reprimanding their mouthpiece, they will be even less inclined to share their true feelings in the future for fear of being the next on the whipping post. It is impossible to work as an effective unit if nobody will share their true feelings and opinions.

Customer Service

Have you ever been hooked by a salesperson whose promises seemed too good to be true only to discover later that they were *indeed* too good to be true?

A project group with a high tech company lost millions of dollars on a contract simply because they wrongly imagined that they knew what the client expected.

The client asked for things that were not part of the existing contract. The group imagined that if they told the client they were unable to fulfill his requests with the allotted resources, he would become upset and possibly terminate the existing contract or refuse to grant the group future contracts. So the group agreed to the client's requests, figuring that somehow they would find a way to satisfy everybody.

Soon it was apparent that the group was not able to make it work after all. In fact as time went by, they got behind... very behind. Rather than say anything, they developed contingency plans to protect themselves in the event the truth was discovered. These contingency plans took up even more time and caused the project to be delayed even further.

Eventually the whole thing blew up, and not only did the company lose the client, but the group was dismantled. Sadly, many people who were extremely talented lost their jobs. The client hired another company, and, ironically, paid even more money to the new company because they were upfront and managed the expectations of what could and could not be accomplished.

This is a classic case of how an entire project fell apart because of people's inability or unwillingness to create an honest relationship by distinguishing between the facts and their imaginations.

So, What's the Problem?

The problem is not that we have assumptions, conclusions, evaluations, and opinions that's a normal part of being a human being. The problem lies in thinking that we are right and not checking in to verify that our imaginations are correct.

The Problem Multiplies

This problem is multiplied further when people do not make sure that what they are imagining about us is correct. How many times have others made wrong assumptions about us? How many times have we not received valuable information because someone imagined we did not need, want, or care to know? Isn't it disturbing to consider how many friendships, business opportunities, or social advantages we most likely have missed because someone misread us?

How can we make effective and clear decisions if the people around us are not telling us the truth or giving us inaccurate information? Remember the statistic at the beginning of Chapter One: 91 percent of people lie regularly.

Because we know that people may not tell us what they are imagining, we often become self-conscious of how we appear, what we say, and how we act. For example, have you ever been afraid to check your watch during a meeting because of what someone might imagine if they saw you? So you wait until you think you won't be observed, and then you sneak a peek at the time?

> In a 1992 presidential debate, George Bush looked at his watch while Ross Perot was speaking. The next day, the media reported that Bush found the debates boring—reinforcing the assumption among some that Bush's heart wasn't in this particular campaign. Bush later said that, in fact, he was not bored with the debates at all. He looked at his watch because he thought that Perot was long-winded and was going over the time limit.

We have covered many examples in which people hurt their credibility, careers, and campaigns for success by not checking in with their imaginations. While most of us won't be running for the office of President of the United States, by simply learning to check in with our imaginations, we can ensure that our own campaigns for success are not easily thwarted.

CHAPTER 3
THE SHOCKING REALITY

While the concept of checking in with our imaginations is a simple one, the actual practice does not come naturally. Checking in with our imaginations would help us to verify whether or not something we believe to be true actually is. However, many people do not do this. Why is that? If checking in will indeed transform our relationships, why don't we just do it? Examining an exercise I routinely perform in my seminars reveals the shocking answer to this question.

How Wrong Are You?

I learned the basis for this exercise from Dr. Brad Blanton.

In this exercise, participants are paired up and take turns sharing what they notice and what they imagine about their partner. Remember, all that we can essentially notice about someone is his or her appearance, actions, and words.

A sample session might go like this:

"I notice that you wear glasses. I imagine you need them for seeing."

Then the other person might say, "I notice that you're not wearing a ring on your wedding finger. I imagine that you're not married."

Then you might say, "I notice that you talk about your co-
workers. I imagine that you really care about what they
think."

Then your partner might say, "I notice that your hand is
touching your face. I imagine that you are thinking."

It is often interesting what people say. I remember one seminar in particular in which I demonstrated this exercise with
a participant in front of the group. After I gave a few examples, I asked the participant, a marketing executive named
Marsha, if she would like to try noticing and imagining
something about me. Marsha responded, "Gladly," and said,
"I notice that you have food on the front of your shirt. I
imagine that you eat like a pig!" So, you never quite know
what someone will say.

Participants do this exercise for the full five minutes without giving any feedback indicating whether their partners
are right or wrong about their imaginations.

Although participants usually have a lot of fun with this,
they quickly realize that it is tougher than they anticipated.
This is because they are being asked to do something they
are not used to doing—verbally sharing what they notice
and imagine about another person.

Further, participants find that it is extremely frustrating to
hear what their partner imagines about them without being
able to give feedback, especially when what their partner is
saying about them is inaccurate.

The reason I do not want them to give feedback to each
other during the exercise is to illustrate the point that they

rarely have a chance to give feedback in life. People usually don't share what they notice and imagine; they just keep it to themselves.

The Results Will Surprise You

After the exercise, participants estimate the percentage of time their partners' imaginations were correct. I invite you to try this with someone for five minutes. Then, share the percentage that you and your partner estimate the other was correct in their imaginations.

If you are like most people in my seminars, this usually averages out to about 80 percent. In other words, in the five-minute exercise, 80 percent of what a person imagines about a partner is correct.

Then I ask, if we are 80 percent correct in our imaginations about another person in a five-minute exercise, what percentage of time do you think we are correct in a lifetime, during which we notice and imagine things about each other all the time? Do you think that the percentage would go up or down?

Participants eventually reason that it would go down. In other words, they believe they would be incorrect about what they imagine about others more often in their overall lives than in a five-minute exercise. You may disagree, but think about it for a moment.

In a five-minute exercise, you would be most likely to choose only the safest and most easily observable assumptions so you don't hurt the other person's feelings or offend them in any way. For example, "I notice that you have a pen in your hand. I imagine you use it to write. I notice that you have loafers on. I imagine that they are comfortable," and so on.

However, in life, we notice and imagine lots of things all the time, many of which we would not share because we are worried that we might be wrong or offensive. So, if the exercise kept going, our imaginations would stretch even further. This would cause imagination to build upon imagination, thus increasing the percentage of time that we are wrong about the other person.

Still disagree? Just consider how often other people are probably wrong about you. It only stands to reason that if people are frequently wrong about us, then we probably are frequently wrong about others as well. Remember, gut feelings can be deceiving, because we tend to remember the times that we are right and forget the times that we are wrong.

So, if we are about 80 percent correct with our imaginations during a five-minute exercise, we could logically predict that in life, throughout which we notice and imagine all the time, the percentage of time that we are correct decreases dramatically. Most seminar participants estimate the figure to be about 50 percent. This means that at least half the time over our lifetimes we are wrong regarding what we imagine about each other.

For example, upon exiting a meeting at work, 50 percent of our thoughts, opinions, and assumptions are likely to be wrong. When another person leaves the meeting 50 percent of his thoughts, opinions, and assumptions are likely to be wrong as well. If each person does not take the time to check in with his or her own imaginations, the result is two different people who received two totally different messages from the same meeting! The worst part about this is that each person may well think he or she is 100 percent right.

Who doesn't love to be right? In fact, we tend to search for things to validate that we are, often missing clues that may point in the opposite direction. To make matters worse, we tend to remember only the times that we *are* right and conveniently forget the times that we are wrong.

When we think we are right, we do not check in with our imaginations, because we imagine that we know what people are really thinking. This is why even though we are aware of the value of feedback, many times we do not pursue it. After all, we have it all figured out, don't we?

For example, I did not check in with my imagination when Mike Tyson said he was afraid to go up in the ring, because I thought that I knew what he was thinking. Clearly, I was wrong.

People will sometimes get defensive about being wrong. What I usually hear is a version of "It is not just me who thinks this way, but others around me." Well, with whom do you hang around and usually choose as friends? If you are like most of us, you tend to choose like-minded friends, people who are similar to you and who think just like you. If that is the case in your life, be careful. You may think you are right more often than you actually are.

So now I can address something that I mentioned in Chapter One: If we have more communication and more ways to communicate than ever before, why does it seem we have more communication problems, not less? The reason is this: If most people truly believe that they are right and others are wrong, and there is an increase in the amount and modes of communication, they will only look for and remember evidence that they are right. In other words, they see what they want to see.

It's Worse Than You Think

When we have problems communicating with people, we withdraw from having interactions with them. If we do this, then we have less to notice, and we will fill in the gap by increasing our imaginings. In relying more on our imaginings, other imaginings are triggered, which in turn trigger even more imaginings. In other words, assumptions trigger more assumptions, ad nauseum, taking us even further away from the facts.

Given that we are 80 percent correct in a five-minute exercise, and maybe 50 percent correct in our lifetimes overall, how correct do you think we are with someone from whom we withdraw our communication, relying more upon our imaginations? Participants in my seminars usually reason that the percentage of correctness would take a significant drop, probably down to about 25 percent or less. In other words, we may be wrong 75 percent of the time.

In a relationship that is filled with issues, we have two people who think they are right but who may be substantially wrong, perhaps 75 percent or more of the time. No wonder we continue to have difficulties and conflicts at work and at home. We all think that we are right, but we have already estimated that we are wrong 50 percent of the time in our lives. Add to that already depressing figure a person with whom we are having a problem, and it is even worse— maybe 75 percent or more.

Whether or not you agree with the percentages, the point is that we are probably wrong more often than we realize. That is actually good news because the more we understand that we *are* wrong, the more likely we will be to check into what we imagine and determine what the facts really are. Thus, we will become better managers, friends, spouses, and so on. We will be empowered to make better decisions with increased confidence.

Some argue that accepting the possibility of being wrong so often would actually *undermine* their confidence, not augment it. This is indeed true, if you derive your confidence from believing that you are right and that others are wrong. However, if your confidence and self-worth are derived from discovering the truth and moving beyond blame, and implementing real solutions, then accepting that you might be wrong is actually a sign of great self-confidence.

A truly confident person is less interested in playing the blame game. He or she is primarily interested in finding solutions. Effective problem-solving involves considering all the facets of a particular problem, not just the ones that a particular individual deems important.

In fact, people who have a hard time admitting that they are sorry or might be wrong are actually insecure and lack confidence. These people allow no room for finding solutions, because they are too busy trying to prove that they are right and that others are wrong. How much conversation and meeting time is wasted with people striving to be right, rather than being willing to check into the facts and discover real solutions?

Putting It Into Practice

We need to check into those imaginations that are negatively affecting our lives. Let's take a look at a few examples of how we would implement this in real life:

"I noticed you have not said anything and I am imagining that you're upset."

"I noticed that this report came in at 5 p.m. instead of the agreed-upon deadline of 3 p.m. I am imagining all kinds of things. What are your thoughts about this?"

Recognizing that there is a 50 to 75 percent chance that we are wrong can have a profound effect. By just checking in with our imaginations about other people and really listening to the answers, the results we desire will be achieved.

> Christi, a software designer who had attended my seminar, approached me in an airport and shared the results she had achieved at home simply by really "getting" that she might be wrong. Christi told me that she had experienced major problems with her teenage daughter, Serena, prior to the seminar. She thought that she was right and that Serena was wrong, so she would constantly lecture her daughter in an effort to impart her wisdom.

Unfortunately, Serena found her mother's wisdom to be questionable and usually tuned out the "nagging."

Deciding to accept the idea that she just might be wrong, Christi thought, "Maybe I *don't* really know my daughter after all." After she returned home, she started asking Serena questions and really listening to her daughter's answers. Amazingly, a whole new daughter showed up! As soon as Serena understood that her mother was *really* listening, she started to ask Christi questions and really listening to those answers as well. Since then, their relationship has been wonderful.

Christi also shared with me that she had implemented this mind-set at work. She realized that she was having problems getting along with people because of her tendency to beat others over the head with her "rightness."

So, using the same method that had been so successful with her daughter, she started to ask more questions, checking into the facts before making decisions. When someone gave her advice, she would really listen from a position that the other person just might have a good point. She reported that this simple technique had put her career back on track. All this success just from discovering that she *might* be wrong!

That is the ultimate irony in what this book suggests: the more you accept that you just *may* be wrong, the better your life will be! Why? Because in adopting this mind-set, you are more likely to ask questions and check into the facts *before* you make decisions. Having all the facts will automatically result in better decision-making skills so that every area of your life will be enhanced.

CHAPTER 4
THE MORE WE UNDERSTAND THAT WE MIGHT BE WRONG, THE BETTER OFF WE ARE

Having worked with thousands of people from different types of industries and organizations, I have uncovered four important keys to delivering difficult messages effectively. Using these keys empowers us to approach any difficult issue and resolve it effectively. These four keys can work together or separately, depending on your need and circumstances. In this and the following three chapters, we will review these four keys in depth.

Key #1: Understanding that we might be wrong

The first key to resolving difficult issues effectively is approaching them with the true belief that we may be wrong—maybe even 75 percent of the time as we discussed in the last chapter.

Let's face it, for the most part, we are lousy actors, and other people are smart. What we really think about a situation comes through loud and clear, no matter what carefully chosen words we use or how much we strive to sound open-minded.

I remember Rachel, an administrative assistant at a major university, who was told by her boss to attend my seminar so she could learn to change her tone. I asked Rachel what kind of feedback she was receiving at work. She replied, "Everyone says that I sound as if I am mad." I asked, "Well, are you mad?" And she said, "Oh yeah, absolutely." I told Rachel that just changing her tone would not work, because that would only be a superficial change. If she were indeed mad, she would still probably sound mad.

It turns out that Rachel was angry because she was overwhelmed at work. As a result, when someone asked for her help, she would get upset.

She used the tools she learned at the seminar and initiated a conversation with her boss, seeking advice and training about how to get all of her work done. Voila! By resolving the source of the anger, she changed her tone and stopped getting mad when people asked her for help.

What we truly believe speaks much more loudly than what we say.

This is why people who go to communication seminars and only learn the "right" words to say without changing the way they think often come across as phonies.

For example, someone learns in a seminar that thanking people for their feedback is a good thing to do. But inside, they really aren't interested in what their colleagues have to say. They may think they are fooling us, but they are only fooling themselves.

Arnold, a manager at a non-profit health organization, complained that his staff was not offering him any feedback. Arnold said he had requested it repeatedly to no avail. When I asked Arnold how he really felt about his staff, he replied, "Well, I think their ideas are stupid." As soon as the words left his mouth, Arnold realized what was causing the problem. His staff sensed that he felt that way about their ideas, and, therefore, were reluctant to provide any feedback.

It's not enough to merely mouth the correct words. We must really believe in the possibility of being mistaken, because it affects our attitudes and the way we communicate. When we accept that we could be wrong, we will approach matters differently.

Now, you may be wondering about the part of your imagination that is correct. Has anyone ever fairly accused you of something that you denied, based solely upon his or her tone of voice? Others will more easily accept the correct part of our imaginations when we approach matters with minds that are genuinely open to the possibility that we might be wrong.

Consider this, with whom would you rather work: someone who thinks that he is right all of the time, or someone who is sincerely open to the possibility that he may be wrong?

The better that we understand that we're often mistaken, the more open-minded we will be and the better we will be able to communicate our point of view.

Here's an example of how it might sound:

"I noticed that I have not received a response to my e-mail asking for feedback on the report. I am imagining all kinds of things; that possibly you did not like the report, or that the information wasn't comprehensive enough. I am probably way off base, so let me just ask you: What are your thoughts about the report?"

You may make it even simpler and say, "I noticed that I haven't heard from you. I have all kinds of thoughts running through my mind. Will you please give me some feedback?"

So, the first key to resolving difficult issues effectively is to approach them with the true belief that we may be wrong, maybe even 75 percent wrong and watch the positive effect that this sincere mind-set has on our communication with others.

CHAPTER 5
TAKING CONTROL OF
OUR OWN ATTITUDE

This chapter explains the second key for delivering difficult messages effectively. Here you will learn some simple steps to help you take control of your own attitude; learn how blame blinds you to the truth; discover how you can become open to solutions; and teach you to deliver the most difficult messages.

A few years ago, I hosted a cable television show. On the show, I interviewed people who were leaders in their fields—corporate executives, business owners, and other experts—to find out their secrets to success.

Although my guests came from different backgrounds, they all had a similar attitude—an attitude of ownership. They took responsibility for and ownership of their lives. They took responsibility for their actions. Not one of these successful people blamed others for his moods, feelings, productivity level, or communication issues.

Key #2: Taking control of our own attitude

The second key to delivering difficult messages so that issues can be effectively resolved is to have an Ownership Attitude. In other words, our attitude is our sole responsibility nobody else's.

Nobody *makes* us think or do anything. We are responsible for our actions as well as our thoughts, opinions, assumptions, and conclusions. They belong to us. We *choose* to think and act a certain way.

When we say:

> *They* stressed me out.
>
> *They* pressured me.
>
> *They* made me do this.

What we are really saying is that "they" control us. It is as if we are saying that "they" crept into our body and made us think and say certain things. Obviously, this is not the truth. We are in control of ourselves. The only way that someone can ever control us is if we give him or her permission to do so. Allowing someone else to control us never improves a situation. Sure, bad things happen, but even if we cannot choose the events that occur in our lives, we can *always* choose our response.

Ever notice that people who perceive that they have no control and who blame others are never really happy? Often, we feel better for a short time when we blame someone. After all, blaming someone else helps get it off our chest. But what happens later? Our misery returns. Why?

Because when we blame others, we relinquish control to do something about the situation to the person that we are blaming. In other words, we are saying that the other person is responsible, so we must wait for them to do something about it.

The only person we can really control is ourself. So if we are going to wait for others to do something about the situation, we might be waiting for a long time… maybe forever.

Blaming others causes us to become close-minded to possible solutions and blind to the ways in which we may be personally contributing to a difficult situation.

> A few days before taking one of my seminars, Gregory, a manager in the services industry, called to inform me that he had recently been demoted because his employees complained about him to the big boss.
>
> Gregory then went on to blame his employees for being unfair and disrespectful. After all, he worked hard and simply expected the same of his employees. He asked, "How could they do this to me?"
>
> I informed him that there was a more useful, but also more difficult question to answer. "Why didn't your employees first approach you with their unhappiness? In other words, what is it about you that made them uncomfortable approaching you first?"
>
> "I don't know," Gregory responded candidly.
>
> I suggested he interview a handful of people and find out.

Fortunately, the people Gregory interviewed answered his questions honestly. They told him, "You never left your office to give us direction and feedback or to find out how we were doing and what we needed. So, we never thought you cared or were interested in helping us out. Plus, whenever we did go to your office, you seemed too busy to talk with us."

Gregory explained that he didn't go outside his office, because he didn't want to micromanage his employees. He imagined that if anyone ever had a problem, that person would come to him. Gregory explained further that he thought his time would be best used in marketing and getting contracts for his office. He imagined that his employees knew this and never thought to inform them. Unfortunately, as he discovered through this feedback, Gregory's preoccupation made him appear inaccessible and unsupportive to the people who worked for him.

Once he recognized what he had been doing to get himself into that situation, Gregory realized this was actually good news, because he could change his behavior and dramatically affect his future. Gregory went to his boss and took responsibility, explaining that he had learned what had contributed to his demotion. He then explained what he would do to change the situation. He and his boss then devised a plan that would allow Gregory to regain his responsibility and stature in the company.

Just as Gregory finally learned, instead of spending our energies second-guessing or blaming others, we need to be concentrating on the one person we can control... ourself.

How Responsible Are We in a Situation?

If you ever doubt how responsible we are for what is happening in our lives, and how much power we have to change things, remember this:

We train and condition people about the way we want to be treated.

> Maria, a public relations consultant who attended one of my courses, took issue with this. Maria said you cannot train and condition everyone. She explained that her husband, Raymond, was building a shed out in the backyard, when, for no apparent reason, he decided to stop building it. Maria complained that it was an eyesore, demanded that Raymond finish the project, and gave him a deadline to do so.

> When the deadline came and went, Maria yelled at her husband and gave him a new deadline. When Raymond ignored that deadline also, Maria was so furious that she threatened him again, telling Raymond that she meant business and that he better get it done. Then, she gave him a final deadline, which he also ignored.

Maria stated, "See, it is impossible to train and condition my husband." Unfortunately, Maria did not like my response. I said, "Yes, you *have* trained and conditioned your husband. You have trained him that your word means nothing."

WE FAIL TO RECOGNIZE THE MESSAGES WE SEND

All of us train people in how to relate to us. However, as with Maria, we fail to recognize that the message we are sending through our actions or inactions often results in a response that is undesirable to us.

I am not suggesting that we should threaten people and then follow through with dire actions. I am, however, suggesting that it is best not to say things that we do not mean or do not plan to carry out.

If we say a report is due by 3 p.m., the person turns it in at 5 p.m, and we do not say anything, we have possibly trained and conditioned this person that our deadlines are not real and that we do not really mean what we say.

In fact, I have found that silence is one way we "train" others to respond to us with an undesirable behavior.

Upon learning this principle, one participant, a banker named John, shared that it was the reason his marriage was having problems. When his wife did something that he didn't like, John wouldn't say anything, hoping that his silence would make a point. Instead, it had the opposite effect, and his wife kept repeating the undesirable behavior.

Likewise, if someone yells at us and we do not say anything, we have just trained this person it is okay to treat us in this manner.

People notice silence and often interpret it as agreement when it is sometimes meant to convey disagreement. That is why so many people who hate conflict and who avoid addressing issues end up creating major conflicts anyway. When we say, "It's no big deal" when it is a big deal, the result is that we train *ourselves* as well as others to deny the truth.

People often train us unknowingly. How often have you intentionally arrived late to a meeting because you knew from past experiences that the meeting would not start on time?

The person responsible for that meeting had trained you and the other attendees that the meeting would start late. It is ironic how meeting leaders who wait to start meetings until enough people show up often train people to be late for future meetings.

> Here is how Anthony, a government official, was able to cure this problem. First, Tony admitted to the staff that he was responsible for the meetings starting late. Second, he emphasized that, in the future, meetings would always start on time, regardless of the number of attendees. Third, he started all meetings at the exact designated time, even if no one was present, and continued through the agenda without any retracing for the late attendees. When the late arrivals requested a review of the missed

information, Anthony refused. This action trained the entire staff about how to deal with Anthony's meetings. It took only a few meetings before everyone began showing up on time.

How are you training people to deal with you? What are you training people at work and in your personal life to do? For example, if you ask people to be honest with you and subsequently become defensive when they do, what happens? Your action, or in this case, reaction, just trained them not to be honest with you. Don't you know somebody who told you he desired your honesty, but your experience with that person has trained you that this is not the case at all?

> Brenda, a participant at one of my seminars, complained that her 19-year-old daughter was lying to her. Brenda explained that she kept demanding that her daughter tell her the truth, which did not seem to work. So I suggested a different tactic. I advised her to go to her daughter and ask her, "What is it about me that makes you feel uncomfortable telling me the truth?" This began to give Brenda insights regarding what she could do differently in order to develop a more truthful and fulfilling relationship with her daughter.

By realizing how much we train and condition people about how to deal with us and by taking ownership of our imagination, we will regain control of difficult situations. Additionally, when we do not blame the other person he will be less likely to become defensive and more open to what we have to say.

So, instead of saying, "You make me think this," say, "I have allowed myself to think this," "I have chosen to think this," "I find myself thinking this," or "I have come to some conclusions about this." The point is that there are lots of ways to convey ownership. Just do it in a style that is right for you.

Here is an example of how it might sound:

"I noticed that you did not say anything in the staff meeting. I have been thinking that you are upset with the situation. What are your thoughts?"

Another example:

"I noticed that you told me the report was "okay." I'm thinking that you're not really that pleased with it. Do you have any feedback to give me about it?"

How to Confront Someone Who May Be Lying

Remember Columbo, Peter Falk's humble and unassuming character from the television show? He had the ability to get anyone to tell him anything. When someone said something that was conflicting or inconsistent, Columbo would rub his head and say, "I notice you said this and now you are saying that. I'm confused," or "Could you clarify this?" or "Help me understand." By taking responsibility for his confusion, he disarmed the other person. That person then felt comfortable telling him things he needed to know.

So, when you think someone may not be telling the truth, remember the "Columbo Method." Stick to the facts, come from the position that you are confused or unclear, give the person the benefit of the doubt, and sincerely ask questions to get clarification.

The Lies We Tell Ourselves Are the Worst Lies of All

How often have you said that you are going to do something, like go on a diet or begin an exercise program, and then not done it? Has it ever reached the point that when you decide something, the little voice inside you chides, "Are you kidding? You will never do it"? Those lies undermine our own confidence to address issues and to effect change. So make sure you are training and conditioning *yourself* to believe yourself. Not telling yourself the truth really hurts only you in the end.

The best way to approach a situation successfully is to take ownership of our imagination and remember that no one *made* us come up with those thoughts, opinions, assumptions, and conclusions we did. Someone else might notice the same facts but draw a different conclusion. By applying Ownership Attitude to our imagination, we will be able to deliver difficult messages so that the issues can be effectively resolved.

CHAPTER 6
MAKE SUGGESTIONS AND CHANGE THE SITUATION INSTANTLY

If a personality conflict, problem, or issue occurs, the challenge of delivering difficult messages can seem impossible. However, difficult messages can be delivered effectively if you first remember the Law of Reflection and use the third key, which is make suggestions to change the situation instantly.

The third key will be discussed in the latter half of this chapter; first, we must review the Law of Reflection.

The Law of Reflection

The Law of Reflection is a universal law that dictates that what we give out is what we tend to get back. Most of us recognize this as the "what goes around, comes around" philosophy. It has also been described as The Golden Rule and "as we sow, so shall we reap." This wisdom is often neglected, and many fail to apply it to their relationships.

When we examine our lives and our careers, this law clearly applies. When others are upset with us, we tend to get upset with them as well. When others blame us, we tend to blame them right back. Others accuse us of something, and we tend to accuse them also. The reverse is true as well. When we take responsibility for our actions, others tend to take responsibility for their actions. When others apologize, we tend to apologize back. This isn't always true, though. Sometimes we apologize to someone and they say, "Well I am glad you finally admitted it." However, even in those situations, their aggression toward us is usually at least minimized.

Whenever I do a seminar for a group that works together, I can usually predict the attitude of a group leader by interviewing the people who report directly to him or her. When they blame, I usually find that the boss is a blamer. On the other hand, when the employees have an attitude of taking full responsibility, I usually find that the boss possesses an ownership attitude as well. The executive's, manager's or supervisors' attitudes seem to be reflected by their employees'. This is often why an organization will make a change in leadership. A change in leadership will directly affect the morale and productivity of a group, even when its members remain the same.

In fact, applying the Law of Reflection is *the* key to compelling people to be more honest with us. The more honest we are, the more likely it is that others will be honest with us. This is not always the case, but it is interesting to note that I frequently hear people complain that there is someone in their lives who is not being completely honest with them. After further discussion, they will almost always admit that they are not being totally honest with the other person either. Sadly, this situation often becomes a standoff in which everyone loses.

A seminar participant named Jane complained to me that her elderly father, with whom she had tried to develop a close relationship, wouldn't ever truly open up to her. I asked her what it was that she was holding back. In other words, what was at the heart of this lack of openness? What was she trying to say, but was avoiding saying by burying it in a lot of words? Suddenly Jane smiled, and said, "I know what it is. I am not sharing with him that I wonder if he approves of the way I am living my life. I have been talking around the issue, hoping that he would voice his approval." Jane also shared that she had avoided confronting her father, because she was embarrassed to admit that she still needed his approval, even as an adult. She left the seminar that day with a plan to tell her father the truth.

Key #3:
Make suggestions and change the situation instantly

The third key to delivering difficult messages so that issues can be effectively resolved is to suggest something that *you could* have done differently (something that might have changed the situation). Let's examine this powerful tool more closely.

This technique is not a sign of weakness, nor does it give unfair advantage to the other party. Rather, it opens the channel for a meaningful dialogue for the following two reasons:

First, I am suggesting that you say **could** have done differently, not **should** have done differently. *Should* implies admitting wrongdoing on your part. Since the purpose of this dialogue is to *solve* a problem, not to determine *fault*, "could" is key here.

Second, when you suggest that you could have done something differently, it actually encourages the other person to suggest things that *he or she* could have done differently as well, which helps *he or she* save face. Why does this happen? Because of the Law of Reflection.

To apply the Law of Reflection in resolving difficult issues, it is important to suggest one thing that we could have done differently, so the other person is likely to do the same. These admitted "coulds" become a potential plan for resolving the issue.

Even if the other person does not rise to the occasion, all of the things that we realize we could have been doing differently become an action plan for the future that is *within our control*.

For example, "I notice that the report came in at 5 p.m. instead of 3 p.m. as we had discussed. I imagine that you had too much to do. One thing I could have done is called you at 1 p.m. and asked how things were going." Now let us say the other person does not take responsibility for his part and says, "Yeah, you should have called me." Then you could say, "Are you saying that next time, if I call to remind you, you will get the report in on time?"

Now, if he agrees, he has just agreed to an action plan that is in your control. And if he disagrees, you can then follow up with, "What do we need to do so that I can count on the report coming in on time?" Either way you are in a position of control. Usually you will find that simply suggesting something you could do differently will cause the other person to do the same.

But I Have Tried Everything...

Do you think that you have already tried everything? Consider this: there are currently over six billion people in the world. Add to that the billions of people who have lived before us. With all those individuals going through lives of their own, the chances are great that *someone* has experienced exactly what we are experiencing and has overcome that obstacle. The trick is to find the answer. Besides, it would be arrogant to say, "I've tried everything and there's nothing I can do," since that is basically saying that never, in the entire history of humanity, has anyone ever faced this same type of problem and fixed it.

However, one thing is certain. If we *think* there is no answer, then we will probably never *see* an answer. As we discussed earlier, we tend to see what we want to see. As Henry Ford once said, "If you believe you can or believe you can't, either way, you'll be right."

This may be hard to see when looking at yourself, but think how often you have watched a friend or a co-worker ignore an obvious solution, even though it is staring them in the face. It is only logical to conclude that we are probably doing the same thing in certain situations.

The Five Percent Rule

Even if you were to conclude that a particular situation is mostly out of your control, (mostly a result of how the other person is acting), just concentrate on your part and watch what happens. For example, let us just say that it was 95 percent the other person and five percent you. Concentrate only on the five percent that you are responsible for. Changing that five percent still empowers you to change the direction of the situation starting now and into the future.

Think of this as a train on a journey, with 100 switches to make before it reaches the end. Our five percent is only five switches but just one switch is enough to take that train to a far different place than where it was originally headed. So let's spend 100 percent of the time on the part we can control.

There is nearly always something we could have done differently which might have affected the outcome of a particular situation. Because of the Law of Reflection, the more we admit to something that we could have done differently, the more others are encouraged to do the same. And then we are on the path to resolution.

Let's look at an example. "I notice that I have not received any feedback about my job performance. I have allowed myself to think all kinds of things. One thing I could have done is to request a time that was good for you to discuss it. So let me just ask you, when would be a good time for us to sit down and talk about my job performance?"

On the personal side, here's another example. "I notice that you don't acknowledge or seem to appreciate me very often. I have all kinds of thoughts about this, and sometimes I feel like you don't care. One thing I could have done was to have been more upfront with you and asked for, rather than demanded, what I want and need. I also could have been kinder and worked on showing you how much I appreciate you." (On a side note, I can't tell you how many times someone complains about not getting enough acknowledgement and appreciation either at work or at home. My response is, "How often do you acknowledge the people that you are complaining about?"). Remember the Law of Reflection: what you put out there is likely to be what you get back.

Since there is likely to always be *something* we could have done differently, suggesting is a natural tool to use, because we can do so honestly. Suggesting, the third key to resolving difficult issues, is an immediate way to get results in your communication with others by taking the focus off the other party and back on to the issue at hand.

CHAPTER 7
STREAMLINE COMMUNICATION

Have you ever been in a conversation with someone who just goes on and on about his or her opinion? Didn't it take every bit of self-restraint not to scream, "Enough!" or "Who cares?"

The fourth key for effectively resolving difficult issues is to eliminate opinions and stick with facts and emotions. In other words, we do *not* necessarily have to share *all* of our imagination.

Key #4: Streamline Communication

I remember Roseanne, a meeting planner, who approached me before the seminar began, and said, "I am glad you are teaching honesty here. We need it. I am honest, and no one likes it." To which I responded, "Well, why don't you give me an example of your honesty?" Roseanne replied, "When I think someone is a jerk, I tell them." I then informed her that we were teaching honesty, not brutality. Name-calling is not really honesty. It is just a cover for how we really feel. In this case, Roseanne felt hurt and disrespected so she lashed out at others.

Nobody wants to hear *all* of our opinions—we have a million of them, and there isn't enough time in the day to express them all. And, as we discussed earlier, there is a 50 to 75 percent chance that our opinions (which fall under the heading of "imaginations" and "imaginings") are incorrect.

So I am suggesting that you do not voice many of your opinions because the other person is probably thinking, "Who cares?"

EMOTIONS

Honesty is about stating facts the way we see them and sharing how we feel about those facts. Sharing our emotions is crucial to helping the other person truly understand our point of view and enlisting his or her help in resolving the situation.

Our emotions are the driving force behind what we say and what we do. For example, when we are forced to work late to complete a project because someone else neglected to complete his or her part, we may feel angry. This anger will drive what we say and how we say it.

Communicating the emotions that drive us: joy, love, hurt, anger, fear, frustration, sadness, or elation is essential to the resolution process. Emotions are how human beings connect with themselves and with others. While individual emotions may differ, we *all* can relate to being motivated by them.

What are your goals? For a goal to be compelling, there must be a set of emotions to drive it. Let us say your goal is to retire to a golf course in Arizona. What is the emotion behind that goal? The joy of spending sunny days on the course? The relief of not working anymore? The relaxation that comes from being able to plan your days the way you want? It is not just the goal of putting in the desert that drives you (so to speak). It is the emotional benefit that you will receive.

Have you ever met someone who did not want to retire? If you ask why, that person will probably tell you he gets a great amount of satisfaction from his work. So, in other words, maintaining satisfaction and enjoyment in life is the driving force behind that person's desire to continue working.

Look at your own life experiences. Around whom do you feel the most comfortable and connected: people who show or discuss their emotions, or those who do not? The former are generally the ones we feel we can trust. What we see is what we get, and we find comfort in this knowledge.

What leaders do we respond to the best? The ones who are willing to show or describe their emotions. The concept of expressing of emotions in leadership is a barrier to some people, preventing them from becoming the great managers they could be. At some point in the past, they were wrongly told to not show emotion in the workplace. Unfortunately, many female seminar participants share that this has happened to them. They were told not to show or discuss emotion at work, and they are now discovering that this actually inhibits their ability to lead effectively.

Remember, we may differ in our experiences and priorities, but we all have emotions. We differ only in our *expression* of emotions and in what it is that we get particularly emotional about. It's a mistake to think that someone is devoid of emotion just because they do not *show* their emotions.

I am not recommending that you explain your emotions or *become* emotional: messy, weepy, and out of control *just that you describe your emotions.* I call this the Tarzan method of communication. Tarzan was a man of few words, yet he was always able to express himself in a way that people understood. So keep it simple and report your emotion: I am mad. I am upset. I am stressed.

For example, we might say, "I notice that you turned in the report three hours after you promised. I'm stressed." We don't have to go on and on, stating *why* we are stressed, or that stress is a big problem in today's society, because the other person is probably thinking, "Who cares?"

> A great example of this is Mark, a purchasing manager at a major corporation, who complained, "My employee, Vincent, is lazy." My response was, "Who cares?" Vincent's laziness was not the point. After more questioning, Mark explained how stressed and upset he was that Vincent was only producing three batches a day, rather than the expected ten batches a day. So, the central problem was that Vincent was not achieving the expected goal.
>
> Obviously, Mark's goal was to get those batches done, but in this case, it was not necessary for him to share his opinions. Why? Because there is a good chance that his imagination is wrong and sharing his opinion could put Vincent on the defensive. As we learned earlier, there is up to a 75 percent chance

that our imaginations are wrong. It's possible that Vincent *was* lazy. It's also possible that he was not reaching his goal because he did not have the budget, tools, help, time, or the training that he needed. Or maybe Vincent didn't remember the agreed upon goals or is poorly suited for the job. Who knows?

I suggested to Mark that he begin the conversation this way, "I notice that we agreed that you would achieve ten batches a day, but currently you are achieving only three batches a day. I am stressed out. My request is that we determine what specifically needs to be done so that you are able to achieve the ten-batch-per-day objective."

It is important for Mark to report his emotion. Although Vincent may not be stressed like Mark is, he knows what stress feels like and can immediately see and relate to his manager's point.

By asking Vincent what needs to be done, Mark can partner with him in creating solutions to achieve the desired goal.

In summary, the most streamlined and effective way to communicate is to state what we notice, eliminate a lot of opinions, and then express our emotions. It is important to remember that we report our emotions because it helps the other person understand where we are coming from, which ultimately helps us get our point across. Plus, there is nothing for the other person to debate because our emotions belong to us, and we are not blaming him or her for making us feel this way.

Here is an example of how this might sound:

"I noticed that we have missed some deadlines this week, and I have allowed myself to get stressed out by this. One thing I could have done differently was to address this issue sooner, without placing blame. My request is for us to figure out specific actions that we can take to ensure this project is completed on time." (Again, focus the conversation on finding solutions, rather than bogging things down with a lot of opinion-mongering).

Expressing Anger

One emotion does require more explanation: Anger. This emotion is frightening to some, even if the angry person is merely reporting the emotion and not demonstrating it. Why?

Anger is a secondary emotion, not a primary one. Therefore, anger is not the total truth. In other words, anger is a result of another emotion, usually hurt or fear.

> Leslie, an account executive at a marketing firm who attended one of my seminars, was mad at a co-worker, Adam, and was trying to understand why. "There's no hurt or fear. I'm just plain mad that he isn't doing his job," she said. It took some talking, but we uncovered the mystery.
>
> Leslie depended on Adam to do his job so that she could do her job. When Adam did *not* do his job, Leslie would have to stay late to pick up his slack, and this took time away from being with her chil-

dren. In other words, Leslie's anger at Adam resulted from her fear that by staying late at work, she was being a bad mother.

I suggested Leslie approach her boss and explain, "I noticed that I am doing other people's work, which causes me to have to stay late and I'm angry. The bottom line is that I am afraid that it is going to affect my personal life by taking time away from my family. My request is for us to devise a specific plan that makes everyone accountable for his own work."

If you still have doubts about expressing your anger, let us examine the options, and you choose which is best. Here are three.

Three Options for Expressing Anger

The first option is to deny anger. For example, someone asks us if we are angry and we say, **"No, I'm not angry!"** Who do we think we're fooling? Denying anger is not useful. It breaks down trust by making people feel deceived. Remember, we are lousy actors, and people are smart. They often have a good idea that they are not being given a truthful answer.

The second option is only to *acknowledge* the anger by saying, "Yes, I am very angry. We don't have enough resources to do my job." This is much better, but the other person may still feel uneasy with our anger, because we are still not stating the total truth regarding the real cause of our anger. Remember? Fear or hurt.

The third option is clearly the most effective. It is to *acknowledge our anger and verbalize the total truth*, to say, "Yes, I am angry. We don't have the resources we need to get the job done. The bottom line is that I am afraid that if we don't take care of this, it will affect my job performance." This way we are not only being truthful, but people can see what is truly fueling our anger. They will therefore have a better idea of what they can do to help.

> A participant in my seminar was extremely upset with a manager at work. Shelia, a researcher at a science and technology company, was told by her manager to go talk to another manager, Rick, about a particular project. When she approached Rick, he immediately cut her off and told her, "I don't talk to people on your level."
>
> After that incident, Shelia was so bothered by what had happened, she avoided Rick as much as possible. In fact, she even used different hallways than she normally did in an effort to avoid bumping into him. Whenever she did see him, she would seethe with anger and think about him for hours afterward. In addition, her attitude and productivity were being negatively affected, and she had stopped liking her job.
>
> When Sheila talked about this encounter in the seminar, she rationalized that there was no need to talk to Rick, because he was obviously a jerk who thought he was superior to everyone.
>
> I told her that this was her imagination talking. She might be right, but she might be wrong. Either way,

it was costing her to have this opinion without checking in and getting clarification. I advised her to have a conversation with the manager.

After the seminar, Sheila approached Rick and said, "I want to talk to you about how we can work better together. I noticed two months ago that you said to me that you don't talk to people on my level. I have imagined all kinds of things. The bottom line is that I have been angry because I am hurt, and I am afraid that it will affect my job. One thing I could have done was to bring this up to you as soon as this happened."

"Oh," he said, "I am so sorry. I wasn't mad at *you*. I thought your supervisor was avoiding me by sending you to talk to me. So I was actually mad at him. I didn't mean to take it out on you, and I am so sorry!"

Two months of personal agony and costs cleared up in minutes by checking in with one's imagination. They not only cleared up the misunderstanding, but Rick eventually became an excellent mentor and trusted friend to Shelia.

In summary, streamlining communication is the fourth and final key to resolving and preventing difficult communication issues effectively. Opinions are subjective and generally not useful in achieving effective communication. While it may seem tempting in the name of "honesty" to bombard others with how we *really* think, a streamlined approach is much more effective.

While it may not seem natural to implement the changes I suggest, it is worth the effort when you count the cost of ineffective communication. Accepting that we might be wrong, taking responsibility for our own attitude, offering suggestions about what we could do differently, and streamlining communication are all effective methods for eliminating ineffective communication. Used in combination, they become a powerhouse with unlimited potential. Remember the Law of Reflection and get to work.

CHAPTER 8
SEVEN TIPS FOR PREVENTING INEFFECTIVE COMMUNICATION

Have you ever been blindsided by a "Big Issue" that just seemed to come out of nowhere? Do you remember how awesome and overwhelming it seemed? While it *seemed* like this "Big Issue" just materialized out of thin air, a closer reflection might reveal warning signs that you overlooked or ignored. Could this have been prevented? Possibly. Most "Big Issues" begin as "little issues." Handled quickly and properly, little issues rarely escalate to "Big Issues."

Tip #1: Forgive

The first tip is to forgive and to let go. In fact, the greatest gift that we can give *ourselves* is forgiveness! Many people think that by forgiving someone, they are in effect letting them off the hook. Not so.

The inability to let go of the past and forgive is often a barrier to attaining true happiness and achievement. This is true both personally and professionally. It has been said that when we harbor unresolved anger and resentment toward someone, we are letting that person live rent-free in our heart and in our mind.

Often, we even rationalize our lack of forgiveness as a way to punish the other person. Sadly, we are only punishing ourselves. There is a cost to this anger, and it exacts a hefty toll on many dimensions of our life.

THE COST OF FORGIVENESS

There are five groups of questions we can ask ourselves to help determine how badly we might be punishing ourselves. Let us refer to this unresolved situation or not-yet-forgiven individual as *Some One*. (For additional questions, check out "The Cost of Communication Breakdowns" in Chapter 1.)

1. How much time am I spending thinking about *Some One*? Has this become my focus? Am I thinking so much about *Some One* that it takes me twice as long to complete other tasks?

2. Do I talk about *Some One* with other people? Do I ramble on about *Some One* and allow this to interfere with my productivity and happiness?

3. Do I have similar problems with other people or situations as I do with *Some One*?

4. Do I lie awake in bed and think about *Some One*?

5. Am I letting *Some One* affect my present relationships? Am I defensive or overly sensitive in a current relationship because I am still sensitive about some past or unresolved issue? Am I afraid history will repeat itself?

If you answered yes to any of these questions, you might consider the advice and insights in the following paragraphs.

Unresolved situations are not only a burden, they are also a distraction. They cause us not to be present and focused on the moment. They can become a constant stress in our life, affecting the quality of our time, relationships, and happiness.

So give one of the greatest gifts you can give yourself: the gift of forgiveness. Forgiveness is essential to free ourselves from yesterday, so we can have a great today. We are not required to *forget*, just to forgive.

WHAT TO DO

Here are three steps for letting go of the past and creating room to forgive.

1. Have a direct conversation with the person. Own up to the fact that you have been hurt by holding onto the past. Then tell him that you forgive him if that's the case. This does not require you to be friends and spend time with the person. Remember, this is about forgiveness, not forgetfulness. You will benefit from doing this face-to-face.

2. Think about the lessons to be learned from the past and commit to specific actions that will help you avoid a repeat performance.

   Example: If you received a bad performance review, ask yourself what lessons you could learn from this. Perhaps the lesson is to be proactive in seeking feedback from your boss, before and during a project; maybe it is to establish and clarify expectations *before* beginning work; or maybe it is to learn that you need to do a better job keeping your boss informed of your progress and accomplishments. Whatever the lessons, identify and acknowledge them. Then commit to doing three things that will directly address and ensure that these situations are not repeated. For example, commit to getting your boss' goals and expectations of you in writing, schedule a regular meeting to review this, and during the meeting, make sure your boss is aware of your accomplishments.

Example: If someone violated your trust, commit to reading self-improvement books, seeing a therapist, and/or taking a course on relationships to determine what you may or may not have done or signs you may have missed. This will help give you the confidence that history will not repeat itself and enable your next relationship to be your best relationship.

3. Create a powerful goal that forces you to leave the past behind.

   Example: After receiving the bad performance evaluation, establish a goal of being promoted or of getting a raise by a specified date (make sure your boss agrees).

   Example: If someone broke your trust, commit to a goal of being in a serious relationship by a specific date. This will cause you to take actions that will help you leave the past where it belongs behind you.

If you ever doubt your ability to forgive someone, just remember Nelson Mandela. Many would say he was entitled to harbor resentment and animosity toward the people who imprisoned him for 27 years, but he did not. He forgave them, and amazingly, many of them participated in his inauguration as president of South Africa. By forgiving freely and completely, Nelson Mandela not only helped himself, he helped an entire nation and in the process saved thousands of lives.

Giving yourself the gift of forgiveness will free you from the burdens of your past and help you excel in the present and achieve in the future.

Tip #2: Find Out What Is Important

What motivates people the most is what is most important to them.

What Do People Want and Value Most?

Who are your customers and what do they want? Remember, our customers are our boss, co-workers, and employees, as well as our spouse, children, relatives, parents, and so on. And some of us have lost our customers.

The key to keeping our customers happy is to know what they want and value the most so we can decide whether or not we can provide it.

When you are working on a project, confirm the criteria for success. Determine what is most important to the parties involved. Be sure that your definition of success is consistent with everyone else's definition of success. Often people work on what *they* think is important, not what others think is important.

> Ginny, a friend of mine, lost her job because she was doing things her way and accomplishing goals that had value to her, instead of asking her boss what he wanted her to do and then doing that. At first she blamed her boss and said, "Well he should have told me what he wanted." And perhaps she had a good point. But the true value of this experience came when Ginny realized she could have asked him. And since she is the only one that she can control, it is better to look at what she could do differently in the future. Ginny could have asked what her boss' expectations were and made sure she met them. Along the way, she could have requested a meeting, asking for feedback rather than waiting for it.

It is impossible to change others but we can change ourselves. By taking responsibility for our own path to success, we take control of our destiny as well.

If They Are Vague

People are often vague when asked what is most important to them. They may say things like, "to do a good job," "to work hard," or "to be sensitive to what the customer wants."

These phrases lack specifics and are too subject to interpretation. It is critical to clarify exactly what they mean. Ask probing questions to establish exactly what is expected.

Here is a list of specific questions that you can ask:

"What are your top three priorities defining the success of this project?"

"Specifically, what is most important to you?"

"When you reflect on this project, what will need to be in place for you to feel that it was a complete success?"

"Paint a picture of how success on this project looks for you."

If someone still has trouble being specific, make some suggestions to help them gain clarity and understanding. And if they really do not know what they want, start by asking them what they *don't* want.

If the person continues to be vague, be patient and ask them if they could be more specific. Explain that this will help you to better serve their wants and needs. Many times people do not realize that they are being vague, and sometimes we are afraid to confront them and admit that we are not sure.

> I remember Scott, a computer systems engineer, who shared that he was concerned about confirming with the client as to exactly what they wanted. Scott said that he was concerned that the client was uncertain themselves and might get upset if he

pressed the issue. I told Scott that he really had no choice. His only other option was to waste valuable time and resources guessing! I assured him that the client would not be nearly as upset by his efforts to seek clarity, as they would be by an incorrect guess regarding their wants and needs.

By finding out what is truly important to the other party, everyone benefits.

Tip #3: Manage Expectations

Relationships fail, opportunities are missed, and much hard work goes unappreciated because of mismanaged expectations.

Once the other party tells you what they really want, be up front regarding whether or not that can be delivered. If the expectations are unreasonable or impossible, tell them. While this may initially upset them, they will appreciate your honesty, and together you can establish reasonable expectations.

Be certain that you are clear regarding what they *can* expect from you as well. For example, you might tell them that you will be honest with them, that even if you are unable to do what they want, you will always tell them this upfront or as soon as you realize it. Shared expectations produce peace and harmony. Be as thorough as possible when establishing expectations and be prepared to adjust as necessary.

Remember the age-old adage "under-promise and over-deliver"? So many hard-working, talented people undercut others' perceptions of the value of their work, because they cannot say "no." They over-promise or do not do what they said they would.

For example, suppose you cannot make a Friday 5 p.m. deadline. You rationalize that calling the customer to let them know will just make them angry. You may further rationalize that nothing would be done with the document over the weekend anyway. Of course, you want to do a great job on the project, and you want to please the customer, so you work very hard and turn it in on Monday morning. But of course, no matter how great the report is, the customer remembers only that it was late. Then you end up deprived of the credit that is due to you, all because of your fear of being direct with the customer at the beginning.

How to Say No Effectively

Say no so that the other person will benefit. Typically, when we cannot do something we say something like, "I am over-worked." We might also say "yes," while resenting the other person, or, worse yet, we say "yes," and then we do not keep our word.

One way to avoid these scenarios is to find a way to say "no" so that the person who is asking you realizes that he or she will benefit by your truthful answers.

For example, you might try saying something like, "I would like to say 'yes,' but I am afraid that if I do, I won't be able to deliver this on time and with the quality it deserves." This, of course, benefits the other person as well as you. This does not guarantee that the other person will be happy, but it is better than your other options that erode trust and make your word appear meaningless.

Make Sure You Clean Up the Past

If you have had a track record of not keeping your promises, admit it to the other party. Admitting it may sound crazy, but remember, they already know. Then promise them that you will keep your word in the future, and, if for some reason you are unable to do so, you will let them know as soon as you know. Finally, if they are still skeptical, you can self-impose some consequences to show them how serious you are. For example, I remember telling someone with whom I worked and to whom I had not kept my promise, that if I did not complete the task, I would give $100 to her.

Managing people's expectations on the front end will eliminate a lot of headaches on the back end.

Tip #4: Have a Relationship Checkup

You need to check up on your relationships periodically, just as you need to go to a doctor for a periodic checkup. This is especially important when you sense problems, such as when you feel someone is not listening, when you are not getting feedback, and/or when you feel you are not getting along with the other person.

Unfortunately, what we often do is just let things go, hoping that time will heal things, and then all will be well.

Remember, if time healed all wounds, we wouldn't have so many people dwelling on things that happened to them years ago and blaming the past for the way things are today.

THREE-STEP CHECKUP FOR RELATIONSHIPS

This is best implemented while you are face-to-face with the person. If you are unable to meet face-to-face, you may do this on the telephone, but please do not attempt to do this by e-mail. While technology is wonderful, there are just some things that need a more personal touch. Here is how it works:

Step 1: Ask any or all of the following questions

On a scale of 1 to 10, how well are we doing? What would make it a ten? A 15 (in other words, over and above)?

Do you think that I listen to you, I mean *really* listen, hear, and understand you?

If you really *don't* listen to the other person, admit it and ask what could be done to improve things. You might think, "Admit it?" Well, they already know it. Can't you tell when someone isn't listening to you? If you feel you *do* listen to the other person, ask them, "How could I prove to you that I really am listening to you?"

If you often place blame, admit it and ask what could be done to improve things. If you don't agree that you blame the other person, ask him or her, "How could I prove to you that I don't?"

Important Notice: It's very hard for people to give honest feedback. So, no matter what they say, *do not debate them.* Just try on their feedback like a shirt. If it fits, use it. If not, discard it. But *before* you discard it, remember the old saying, "If three people call you a horse, you better start looking for a saddle." If you get defensive, there is probably some truth to it, or you may be *afraid* that it is true. If it weren't true, it probably wouldn't be so upsetting.

Step 2: Make commitments

Unilaterally, commit to some action that you will take to improve the relationship. This will encourage him or her to take action as well, and things will improve (remember the Law of Reflection). For example, you might tell the other person that from now on, you will admit when it is a bad time to talk instead of pretending that everything is okay and pretending to listen.

Step 3: Follow up

Plan a time to follow up with the other party to check how things are going. Choose an appropriate method of following up: telephone call, lunch, dinner, cup of coffee, etc. When following up, go back to Step 1. Repeat these steps as needed.

The realizations gained by conducting this checkup can be profound.

> Thomas, a man in my seminar, was complaining that his teenage daughter, Amanda, wasn't listening to him. So I asked Thomas if he was listening to her. He grinned and admitted that he was not. Then I

asked him the likelihood of Amanda listening to him if she feels he isn't listening to her. After careful consideration, Thomas agreed that it was unlikely that his daughter would listen to him until she felt he was indeed listening to her. So, he decided he would go home, admit to Amanda that he wasn't listening and ask what he could do to improve things.

The same is true of the people in our lives. Until they feel heard by us, it is unlikely that they will be willing to hear what we have to say. By using the simple Three-Step Relationship Checkup and teaching others to do the same, we can dramatically alter our relationships with one another, producing the results that we want and eliminating big communication issues down the road.

Tip #5: Listen for the Real Message

I know I am a little biased, but the most terrific woman I know is my mother. She has helped by giving me advice that has empowered me to avoid many problems. Unfortunately, as embarrassing as this is to admit, I missed out on many years' of my mom's wonderful advice. Why? Because I was missing the real message.

My mother, by her own admission, can be extremely negative. If I say things are going wonderfully, she might say, "but are you prepared for the future?" I have run my own business for more than 12 years and every year, she reminds me that April 15 is tax day and to be prepared. There are many things that I may be in danger of forgetting, but that date is not likely to be one of them. If there is a possible negative outcome to *any* situation, Mom will be the one predicting it and advising me how to save my behind.

So, because my mom can be negative, for years I missed the real message behind her advice. I heard her negativity and devil's advocacy as a form of disrespect. I reasoned that if she really respected me, she would not be the voice of doom, constantly warning me about such things. I was an adult, after all, and I was offended that she had so little faith in my instinct for survival and my business acumen.

Then, one day, I took a seminar in which the leader said to remember to listen for the real message, that sometimes the true message lies *behind* the words. At that moment, the light bulb went on in my head. My mother was doing this because she cared! In other words, voicing her worries was a form of expressing her love for me, not a form of disrespect. Boy, did I feel stupid and embarrassed.

From that moment forward, I have vowed to hear the real message that my mom is trying to communicate. In other words, I hear my mom's worries and warnings as a form of love and her way of continuing to take care of me, and I now realize how terrific and wise she is and always has been.

Is there someone in your life whose real message you may be missing?

Whether it is a client, coworker, or someone in our personal life, it is amazing how easy it can be to miss the real message. Remember you cannot change people, but you *can* change the way you choose to hear them.

When someone complains, do we hear just the complaints or do we take the time to recognize the message behind the complaints? Perhaps he or she is very dedicated to the job and wants to excel but feels frustrated by a lack of resources. So, the person   complains rather than asking for what he or she wants. While this is not a very effective method of communicating, it can be much less distressing for the listeners if he/she remembers to look for the real message behind the complaining. *Remember: the opposite of love is not hate. It is indifference.*

Complaining clients who are hard to work with can become our best, most loyal clients if we turn them around. If they truly did not want to make things work for us or if they really *had* given up, they probably would remain silent and just try to end the relationship. We can use these opportunities to train ourselves to really listen to the other party.

There may be a lot of people saying important things, but if we are not careful to listen for the real message, we will miss it.

Tip #6: Understand the Purpose

Whenever someone walks into your office, calls you on the phone, or sends you an e-mail, your overriding question is, "What's the point of this communication?" "What's the purpose?"

It is important that someone with whom we are communicating understands our purpose for the contact. This may seem obvious, but how often have you left a meeting or received an e-mail that seemed to be without purpose? It may be common sense, but is it common *practice*?

There are three benefits to informing someone of the purpose for a discussion or confrontation:

1. **Understanding** It helps the other party understand *why* we are addressing the issue in the first place. As someone once said, "People do not care how much you know until they know how much you care."

   Say, for instance, we have the issue of missed deadlines. Why are the missed deadlines important? Maybe they are affecting the overall quality of the project, which we may be concerned will affect future contracts and work. So, the purpose of our addressing the subject of missed deadlines may be that we want the completed project to be the highest possible quality and to ensure future contracts with that particular customer. In making this clear, the other party is then able to understand why we are bringing up the subject of the missed deadlines. In other words, we are addressing the subject because we are trying to do the best job we can, not just complaining. Clarifying our purpose puts the other person at ease. In the above example, our motivation for quality, not criticism, becomes clear, paving the way for productive and comfortable problem-solving discussion.

Again, this *seems* obvious, but how often have you been in the middle of a heated discussion because one or both parties have lost sight of the purpose for the encounter?

Have you ever met someone who may be a little brusque, but you are okay with how they talk to you? Have you ever met someone who says all the appropriate things, but somehow they bug you any-way? In the latter case, you may question their pur-pose. In the former, you may think that though they do not say things in the best way, they are really looking out for you. In other words, you feel like you really understand his or her purpose.

2. **Commonality** Purpose often establishes commonal-ity between you and the other person. This is because the purpose or what you want out of the situation should be what the other person wants as well. And if they are in alignment with your purpose, they will be more likely to help you find a solution.

For example, if the purpose of your addressing an issue is so that you can work more effectively with another person, chances are that the other person wants the same thing.

3. **Direction** Purpose gives direction to our communication. If we have a clear idea of what the desired outcome is, our conversation will more likely be headed in that direction.

Here is an example of how this process may sound:

"I want to talk to you about how we can make this project the highest quality possible. I noticed that we have missed some of the deadlines, and I have allowed myself to get stressed by this. One thing I could have done was to address this issue when I first noticed it. My request is for us to iron out specific steps that we could take to ensure that we complete this project on time, with the customer being extremely happy."

Tip #7: Explain the Benefit

Whether you want to obtain new business, sell your employees or boss on an idea, or want your spouse to fulfill your request, remember the universal language we all speak in is "what is in it for me."

But here is the problem. When someone asks us to do something, we usually evaluate it and think what is in it for us. When we ask someone else to do something, we usually think about what is in it for us. That is the problem, we usually think about what is in it for us, even when the key to getting things in our life is what is in it for "the other person."

It is remarkable how many times I have encountered people who complain about not getting something and then they will explain, "I can't believe that person doesn't realize how much that affects me." Well of course we will not be persuasive if our focus is on us. In fact, we will get what we want when the other person realizes that there is something in it for them.

Want a raise? What is in it for your boss? Want someone to assist you on a project? What is in it for the person? Want someone to turn in some paperwork on time, turn in a time sheet on time, or come to a meeting on time, think about what would be in it for the other person.

One of the top reasons why people are not as persuasive as they could be is that they are not thinking about what would be in it for the other person. In fact, it does not require so much training as it does just being more oriented to thinking of it from the other person's position. For example, without any training, children are extremely persuasive. Why? Because they quickly realize in order to get what they want, others must realize how they will benefit. Notice how children will say if you do this, "I will love you more," "I will clean up my room," and of course my favorite, "I will stop bugging you."

Participants in my seminars often ask me what do I do in economic times like this. My response is to do the best job you can. Nothing can give you 100 percent job security, but the better job you do, the less likely you are to be laid off, because there is an incentive for the organization to keep you. And even if you are laid off, it will be easier to get a new job if you have done a great job.

So when you are thinking about asking someone to do
something, whether in your business or personal life, think
about what is in it for them and remember 7 benefits that
drive human behavior—"MT. SAMIE"

M Money As Zig Ziegler once said, "Money isn't
everything, but it ranks right up there with
oxygen."

T Time It is staggering how many people are time
impoverished. For example, see if your request
will help eliminate wasted time, as in repeated
discussions or meetings.

S Security People tend to avoid risk in search of
security. One example of security as leverage is
job security.

A Achievement We like producing results. So if
your request will help someone else accomplish
something they have wanted to achieve, you will
grab their attention. For example, if your request
would also help your boss achieve your boss' goals,
then you will be more likely to grab his or her
attention.

M Making a difference People will work hard if they
feel like they could really make a difference. Look
what is happening in our country today. People
will often help out if they feel like what they are
asked to do will really make a difference. This is
why I think so many organizations have a problem
with paperwork. They have not explained how
the paperwork requested will be used and the
difference it makes.

I **Image** We are all concerned about what others think. We often just lie about it and say, "I don't care what they think" when often we really do. The power of image is why so many of us have a hard time saying "no." So if your request affects someone's image, then you will likely capture their attention. For example with someone with whom you are having a lot of issues, you might tell them how much you hear other people talking about the two of you, and so if you could just resolve the issues, it might improve both of your images.

E **Enjoyment** People will go to great lengths to have more enjoyment in their lives. Remember if you are not enjoying the situation you are currently in with someone, realize they are probably not enjoying it either. So the "what is in it for the other person" would make things less stressful and more enjoyable. (Children are experts at this one :-)

"MT. SAMIE" is not about manipulating the other person. It is about actually respecting the other person. And rather than complaining because someone is not cooperating with us, agreeing with our point of view or giving us what we want, think and then talk about with them what might be in it for them to do what you would like. And if you are not sure, you could always ask.

Some of this may seem obvious but remember common sense doesn't necessarily mean common practice. After all, when was the last time someone made a request of you and told you what would be in it for you?

So remember the universal language we all speak; it is the key to getting what you want.

Summary

By exercising forgiveness, finding out what someone wants, managing expectations, proactively inquiring about other issues, making sure someone knows your purpose, and explaining the benefits, you can avoid the "Big Issues." This will allow you to invest your valuable time in what you want and need to accomplish.

CHAPTER 9
IF YOU FORGET EVERYTHING ELSE, REMEMBER THIS...

We have addressed a number of techniques in this book that will make a difference in the way you communicate. They *will* produce results. However, there is *nothing* more important than remembering to acknowledge and appreciate people. It is the greatest gift that you can give someone!

My grandfather, Giulio Oreffice, lived in a nursing home during the last several years of his life before passing away at the age of 99¾ years and one day. During one of my visits to see him, a nurse pulled me aside and told me what a "great man" my grandfather was. Appreciative, I asked her why she thought so. She responded, "He is the only person here who always says 'thank you.'"

Wow, just two words in the English language! That does not seem like a lot, but it means so much, and to this nurse it meant everything.

My grandfather always acknowledged people. He acknowledged small things, as when, during my last visit with him, he thanked the nurse for helping him with his hearing aid. He acknowledged large things, such as his referring to his daughter, my mother, as an angel for visiting him daily and making him feel loved and inspired to face the challenge of another day.

We do not have to throw a party or organize an awards ceremony, although it never hurts. We just need to acknowledge and appreciate people.

Why is acknowledgement so important? I believe that the number one driving force of human beings is our desire to make a difference. We want to see that our lives count and we need to feel like we *matter* to someone, that we are noticed and important. To acknowledge someone is to say, "I **see** you. You are significant. I admire you." Who doesn't need to hear these things?

Many of us work extra hours, often for no additional money or benefit. Why? Because we just want to make a difference in our jobs or by helping someone out. That is why many of us have a hard time saying "no." In fact, in conducting career development seminars, I have learned that one of the biggest fears that all people seem to have in common is dying without making a difference. Those of you who are parents know exactly what I am talking about. Parents worry: Are we really helping our children to become the kinds of people that they have the potential to be? Are we equipping them for the future? Are we making a difference?

Some people ask me, "Is it possible to over-acknowledge people?" Perhaps, but the issue is more likely to be the *quality* of the appreciation—whether our sincerity is in the acknowledgement—not whether there is too much of it. In fact, I have never heard of someone leaving an organization because he or she was acknowledged too much. I have never heard of anyone ending a marriage because there was just too much love and appreciation. I have never heard of a child growing up dysfunctional because the child was acknowledged too much. But, of course, we have all heard of people leaving organizations, ending marriages, and remaining upset about their childhoods because they were not acknowledged enough.

The Key to Acknowledgement

When it comes to acknowledgement, I try to remember the "ISOS" acronym.

I **Immediate** Even if it is over the phone or e-mail, express it now. (You can always do something really special for them later).

S **Specific** What specifically are you acknowledging?

O **Often** We already have determined that you can-not harm someone by over-appreciating them.

S **Sincere** Say it only if you mean it.

THE BEST TIP

If you want to do something really special and memorable for someone, buy a card and write down the lessons you have learned from having him or her in your life and then give it to that person. The written word allows for a degree of candor and a level of boldness that face-to-face conversation sometimes does not.

Give the greatest gift that you can give someone: Give the gift of acknowledgement and tell someone what a difference he or she has made in your life. Then watch the difference *you* make in *someone else's life*, just by acknowledging this truth.

CHAPTER 10
SOME FINAL THOUGHTS

"No legacy is so rich as honesty"

– William Shakespeare

Honest communication cannot only help you to resolve issues, but it is also a way for you to build trust with people. And trust is the foundation of all relationships.

As you become skilled in distinguishing what you notice from what you imagine, you can help other people do the same (remember the Law of Reflection).

This can be a real gift for the people you care about: your friends, family, and co-workers who may be struggling with their thoughts and feelings and letting those thoughts and feelings become obstacles to their success in work and relationships.

Do you need to use everything that we have talked about? The answer is no. If you try to use everything, you will likely wind up not using *any* of it. As you read this book, there were bound to have been certain scenarios that resonated with you. Review these scenarios, take the techniques offered, and put them into practice. Begin by trying to make one small change in the way you relate to others.

Finally, I would like to leave you with these four points:

1. The secret to communicating and working effectively with anyone is honest communication. When
   you create an environment that fosters and supports
   honest communication, every dimension of your life is
   improved.

   The most critical strategy in honest communication
   is to distinguish between what you *notice* and what
   you *imagine*.

   At least 50 percent of our unchecked imagination
   is wrong. That percentage increases when conflict
   exists and we reduce the amount of communication. When we reduce interaction, people often fill
   in the gap with incorrect assumptions and opinions.
   Hence, we need to check into our imaginations by
   asking the other person for clarification, and when
   appropriate, expressing our imagination. This helps
   us to focus our time and resources on resolving the
   real issues.

2. When resolving difficult issues:

   - Say it with the true belief that you might
     be wrong

   - Take ownership of your attitude

   - Say one thing that you could have done
     differently

   - Stick with the facts, omit opinions, and report
     your emotions

3. When trying to prevent big communication issues:

- Forgive

- Find out what is important

- Manage expectations

- Do a relationship checkup

- Listen for the real message

- Know the purpose of the message

- Explain the benefit

4. It is not how smooth you are, it is how sincere you are that matters. Some people can be articulate, but they may not be credible. Others stumble over their words, but they are so compelling and endearing in their sincerity that they win friends and supporters everywhere they go. So remember, you do not have to be perfect; you just have to be sincere.

Checking into your imagination allows you to benefit from corrections, which creates a more open environment in which people are more likely to collaborate with one another. This collaboration leads to shared information and ideas. New opportunities can be seized, new levels of excellence can be achieved... and you can produce the results you want.

About the Author

Steven Gaffney is an expert communicator, however this was not always the case. At the age of three, he could only mumble a few words. A doctor told his mother he should be put in classes for "mentally retarded" children. She did not accept this. Doctors eventually discovered that Steven's inability to speak was caused by correctable hearing impairments. After several operations, Steven's hearing problems were corrected, but he was still unable to communicate. His mother took him to Easter Seals for speech therapy. They taught him to speak, and no one has been able to silence him since. Today, Steven Gaffney is an inspired presenter on the topics of communication, motivation, and leadership. Lesson learned: *While most of us are able to speak, many of us struggle to communicate.*

He has developed and refined the **Honest Communication Results System™**, a simple, effective method of communicating that will enable you to speak to anyone, about anything, at any time.

Steven Gaffney is a member of the National Speakers Association and presents frequently to many major corporations and organizations. His clients include American Express, Marriott, IBM, the National Education Association, Meeting Planners International, American Cancer Society, Environmental Protection Agency, NASA, Department of the Treasury.

His programs consistently receive the highest marks, and his attendees report immediate, sustainable results. He has been interviewed on numerous radio and television shows, and his name has appeared in *The Wall Street Journal*, *The Washington Post*, and *USA Today*. He was an adjunct faculty member of The Johns Hopkins University, as well as a past board member of the Washington, D.C. Chapter of the Sales and Marketing Executives International. He produced and hosted his own cable access show, *Maximum Effectiveness*, and in 1995, he founded POWER—People Organized for World Empowerment and Results, a 503(c) non-profit volunteer organization that provided speakers and trainers to charitable organizations for four years.

Steven is continually developing materials to help individuals and organizations realize their full potential. His commitment is results, and he won't rest until the results you desire have been achieved.

How to Contact Us

Steven Gaffney and his company offer keynote addresses, seminars, and consulting services. His **Honest Communication Results System**™ and his popular seminar, "The Fish Isn't Sick... The Water's Dirty," have produced extraordinary results.

To find out more about Steven's programs and products, visit his web site (http://www.StevenGaffney.com) or call toll-free at 1-877-6-Honest (1-877-646-6378).

He looks forward to hearing from you. Please share your results with him. After all, he may need material for his next book!

How to Receive Monthly E-Mail Tips

Steven Gaffney's *E-mail Tip* is a free, monthly service to help you remember the valuable information he teaches. If you would like to directly receive these tips, please sign up on our web site at www.StevenGaffney.com.

Recommended reading

Career and Life Development

Living, Loving, Learning by Leo F. Buscaglia.

The 7 Habits of Highly Effective People: Powerful Lessons in Personal Change by Stephen R. Covey.

Think and Grow Rich by Napoleon Hill.

Using Your Brain for a Change by Richard Bandler.

Emotional Intelligence by Daniel Goleman.

It's Not Over Until You Win! by Les Brown.

Organization, Time and Priority Management

First Things First by Stephen Covey, Roger Merrill and Rebecca R. Merrill.

How to Get Control of Your Time and Your Life by Alan Lakein.

Getting Organized by Stephanie Winston.

Organizing from the Inside Out and *Time Management from the Inside Out* by Julie Morgenstern.

General Communication

How to Argue and Win Every Time by Gerry Spence.

How to Get Your Point Across in 30 Seconds or Less by Milo Frank.

How to Run a Successful Meeting—In 1/2 the Time by Milo Frank.

Delegating and Personality Responsibility

The One Minute Manager Meets the Monkey by Kenneth
Blanchard, William Oncken and Hal Burrows.

Becoming More Open and Honest

*Radical Honesty: How to Transform Your Life by Telling the
Truth* by Brad Blanton. (Caution: This publication
contains language that some readers may find offensive).

The Truth Option: A Practical Technology for Human Affairs
by Will Schultz.

Negotiating Without Manipulation

Getting to Yes: Negotiating Agreement Without Giving In
by Roger Fisher and William Ury.

Asking Questions for Better Results

Smart Questions by Dorothy Leeds.

The Book of Questions by Gregory Stock.

Motivating Other People to Take Action

Empowerment Takes More Than a Minute by Ken Blanchard,
John P. Carlos and Alan Randolph.

Gung Ho!: Turn on the People in Any Organization
by Ken Blanchard and Sheldon Bowles.

Fun in the Work Place

*Nuts! Southwest Airlines' Crazy Recipe for Business and
Personal Success* by Kevin Freiberg.